THE
Archive Photographs
SERIES

SHIPLEY
AND WINDHILL

Fox Corner c. 1920. A scene at the intersection of Shipley's two main highways just after the First World War.

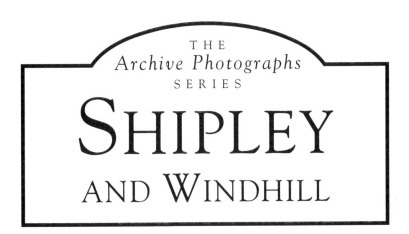

THE
Archive Photographs
SERIES

SHIPLEY
AND WINDHILL

Compiled by
Dr Gary Firth

CHALFORD

The Chalford Publishing Company
St Mary's Mill, Chalford,
Stroud, Gloucestershire, GL6 8NX

ISBN 0 7524 0615 9

Typesetting and origination by
The Chalford Publishing Company
Printed in Great Britain by
Redwood Books, Trowbridge

*For two Shipley lasses,
Clara and Dorothy Armstrong*

Shipley in 1900, a postcard celebration of the town's major landmarks at the turn of the century.

Contents

The Yorkshire Penny Bank, Otley Road in 1937.

Introduction

Although Shipley merits a mention, as early as 1086, in William I's Domesday Survey, and is recorded in numerous documents throughout the Middle Ages and the Industrial Revolution, the focus of this book is on the development of the town and its satellite communities during the twentieth century. Presented here is a collection of images which date from Edwardian times, when Shipley was enjoying the fruits of a successful industrial economy based principally upon textile production, to more recent times.

Shipley's position at the junction of the highway from Skipton to Leeds (Airedale) and from Otley to Bradford (Wharfedale), and its very early location as a rare fording point for the River Aire, all contributed to its original settlement site which is sheltered on the east by the millstone crags of Wrose and Windhill and to the north by the wind swept moors of Baildon and Hawkesworth. Shipley is situated within the parish of Bradford and by 1700 was a small but thriving independent manor owned by the Rawson family. The small farming township of three principal highways (Kirkgate, Westgate and Hall Lane) was surrounded by unenclosed fields at Shipley Fields and the Hirst and by the waste land of the High Moor (Nab Wood and New Close) and Low Moor (Wycliffe).

One hundred years later in 1800, we have a reasonably accurate picture of the geography of Shipley and its environs from an actual map made by J. Fox, a Bradford land surveyor at the end of the eighteenth century (viz p.8). By this time the town was linked to the national canal network following the construction of the Leeds–Liverpool Canal. The trout-filled Bradford Beck ran alongside the steeply sloping pastures of Shipley fields which provided an idyllic setting for Shipley Low Hall. Between Hall Lane and the Otley Road and parallel to them, one can make out the farm occupation road of Croft House (probably the line of later Dale Street). The Market Place was located at the intersection of all the major roads through the town. Finally, the map clearly illustrates a number of substantial yeoman houses built in Shipley after the 1600s: the Manor House (1673), Old Hall (1593) Low Hall and Shipley Hall (1734).

These halls and the families who lived in them, monopolised the affairs of the town, as well as the backward farming economy, until well into the nineteenth century. This ancient way of life was broken after 1814 when the common lands were enclosed and after 1856, when the Lord of the Manor obtained a special act of Parliament which allowed him to sell his Shipley estates for building purposes and thus irrevocably transforming the physical layout of the town. The sudden availability of land in the town centre coincided with the arrival of the Midland railway (1844) and the building of the gasworks (1846). A vigorous and expanding domestic textile trade later caused the establishment of several mills for woollen and worsted cloth production. In addition, coal and ironstone had been mined at Shipley since 1600, principally at Northcliff and Cottingley High Moor. Stone quarrying and tanning were also major occupations in the town before 1800.

As employment prospects improved so did the town's population, rising from 1,400 in 1801 to 3,272 in 1851. Originally only small numbers of people had lived close to the town centre, others were spread more thinly – from as far afield as Hirst Wood, Moor Head and Frizinghall. Increasingly however the town's new cloth mills including Well Croft required a workforce close to the centre of production and consequently rows of terraced cottages emerged within the traditional town centre. Joseph Hargreaves had rebuilt Well Croft Mill and filled ancient yards and folds, such as Spurr's Yard and Hudson Fold, with cheap housing for his operatives. These squalid back to back cottages in Chapel Lane and Low Lane, adjoining the canal, had become a serious health problem by 1850. Three years later, Shipley was constituted as a separate local government district with an elected board of members to oversee public health matters. Only three sewers drained the whole town discharging their effluent into Bradford Beck and into a slough near Crowghyll. In time, drains were laid, roads improved, a water supply provided and the streets illuminated and policed. In 1874 a School Board was elected for Shipley and new schools were built. Of public buildings there were few before 1850. Shipley was part of the parish of Bradford and did not warrant its own Anglican church until 1826 although a small Baptist chapel, Bethel, was built at Low Well in 1758. The old Manor House served as a municipal headquarters in 1880 and eleven years later Windhill Board was amalgamated with Shipley in 1894 and the Shipley Urban District Council (come back all is forgiven !) came into being.

Shipley's nineteenth century growth and prosperity were transformed after 1853 with the decision of Titus Salt to build his huge mill within Shipley's boundaries. There followed the building of over 800 houses (accommodating 4,500 persons) and numerous public buildings including a factory school, an institute and hospital all located in rural sites soon to be overrun by Shipley's own urban sprawl after 1880, when the appearance of modern Shipley is complete. The absorption of Windhill to the east of Shipley in 1894 had counterbalanced the inclusion of Saltaire in the 1860s to create a community in 1900 of 25,600 persons. In 1885 Shipley was the head of a new parliamentary constituency and its first ever M.P. was Joseph Craven.

Although still very much a 'wool town' around 1900, Shipley's industrial base became more varied: Lee and Crabtree (later Metal Box) came as loom makers, later, in 1914, going on to make plant and press tools; W.P. Butterfields made galvanised containers in their premises at Low Well which were once occupied by loom makers David Sowden and Sons; Parkinson and Sons, machine tool makers, originally came to Shipley as engineers to the textile industry. In the 1930s came a third wave of industrialisation: the jam makers, sauce makers and greetings

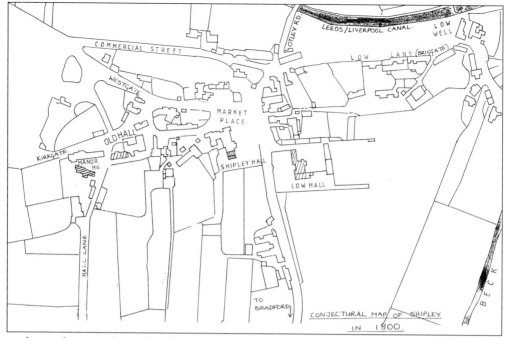

Conjectural map of Shipley in 1800.

card manufacturers. In 1945 industry in Shipley braced itself for the uncertainties of a post-war economy and the town committed itself to removing the last of its Victorian slums with a massive central area redevelopment programme.

The renewal of the town centre in 1955 and 1956 meant the clearance of old shops and streets from Shipley's Victorian past but it also meant the demolition of several fine, ancient yet sturdy homes and farmhouses from the town's pre-industrial past. By 1960 the town centre had changed beyond all recognition and the photographs in this book have been selected to reveal that change, as well as to trace the town's historical development. The photographs are the work of professional and amateur photographers alike. Of the latter, one deserves special mention. Bill King was a gifted amateur photographer and the section on Windhill is dedicated to his memory. I hope that the book evokes something of the atmosphere of Shipley in the old days and brings back memories for older inhabitants, as well as being a source of information for those new to the town.

Gary Firth,
Windhill,
December 1995

Acknowledgements

Grateful thanks are extended to all who loaned or supplied photographs for this book, in particular Ian Watson and Dorothy Sharp of the Shipley Local History Society; Keith Davies, Dorothy Burrows, Nick Jefferies, Kenneth & Dorothy Firth, Paul Osbaldiston, Percy Price, Paul Teale, Frank Woodall, *Telegraph & Argus* and the planning department staff at Shipley Town Hall. A special thankyou to Margery Baker for allowing me access to her father's (Bill King) photographic collection. Finally, my thanks to Jen Godfrey for secretarial help.

One
Edwardian Shipley

The road leading from Shipley to the model village of Saltaire in 1901.

Fox Corner Shipley 1903. Another view of this busy junction dominated by horse-drawn carts of precariously packed woollen bales and the old Fox and Hounds, of mine host, Charley Pickard.

Briggate, c. 1900. The young man looks in the direction of the Midland Bank, Queens' Palace Theatre and the Fleece Inn. Behind him are the premises of J. Brown (menswear and hatters). At Fox Corner is Mr Dunn's chemist shop. The prevalence of horse transport is obvious on the cobbled street before him.

Commercial Street in 1890. Perhaps the oldest photograph in this book. The ancient appearance of these shops prior to their modernisation in 1899 gives us an idea of how Shipley had looked for most of the Victorian period.

Commercial Street c. 1908. The old highway has been transformed and widened to meet the needs of the new transport technology and the growing township. To the left are new shops of retailing chains like Freeman, Hardy and Willis, Maypole and Horne Bros.

Briggate c. 1905. Formerly Low Lane or *Low Loin*, this old road to Leeds and Windhill has also been overtaken by the electric tram system and the retailing revolution. To the left, on the corner with Otley Road are the premises of the Yorkshire Banking Company (formerly London & Midland Bank). Further along Briggate can be seen the 'twice nightly' advertisement of the Queen's Palace Theatre.

Briggate 1908. Another view of the same stretch of road but looking back towards Fox Corner. The gentleman on the left stands outside the shop window of Mr Smith's general drapery store. Smith, who was declared 'the father of Shipley tradesmen' had first begun in business in Saltaire road in 1870. Nine years later he moved to Briggate where he expanded to become Shipley's 'great provider of clothing' in a block of four shops at the corner of Briggate and Charles Street where they still retail a hundred years later.

Low Well, Shipley. Further along Briggate, in the direction of Leeds, the road drops steeply and bends sharply, outside the ironworks of David Sowden's loom makers (later Butterfields). Across the road are the premises of John Wilcock and Sons, corn dealers and flour merchants. Far left is Chapel Lane leading up to the Baptist Chapel on Bethel Hill.

Westgate 1897. A view of one of Shipley's oldest streets taken from Rosse Street. The property on both sides of the road has survived but the buildings in the centre (Cricketers Arms) made way for a new Market Hall in 1956. On the extreme right of the picture is Atkinson's millinery shop and next door is Ainsworths' tailoring establishment.

Market Place 1903. Shipley's ancient marketing centre was located at the junction of the town's principal roads, Kirkgate, Westgate and Otley Road. Off the Market Place to the left is Kirkgate and Market Street. The large building on the right is the Sun Hotel which overlooks the entrance into Westgate where the Albion Drug Stores can be seen alongside the hotel.

Market Place 1912. A similar view of the market place taken only a decade later but with a clear view of the boot and shoe emporium of Mr Lupton Brook in Kirkgate, and Scuhler's pork butchers (with the sun blinds) in the centre. Along Westgate, John Driver's green grocers can be spotted and on the extreme right are the Sun Vaults overlooking the railway line. The Market Place by 1912 has a new public water fountain in place of the public stocks (Stocks Hill).

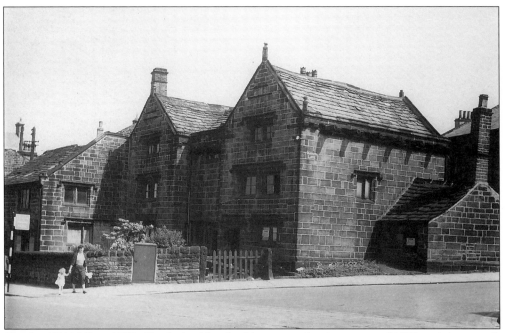

Shipley Old Hall in 1955. Shipley's oldest building carried a date stone of 1593 and the initials J D, A D are thought to be those of John and Anne Dixon. By 1900 it served the town as a model lodging house and shortly before its demolition in 1956 was divided into three cottages. In the second photograph can be seen the rooftop finials which denote the connection of this site with the Order of the Knights of St John of Jerusalem. The house was located at the junction of Kirkgate with Manor Lane (formerly Hall Lane).

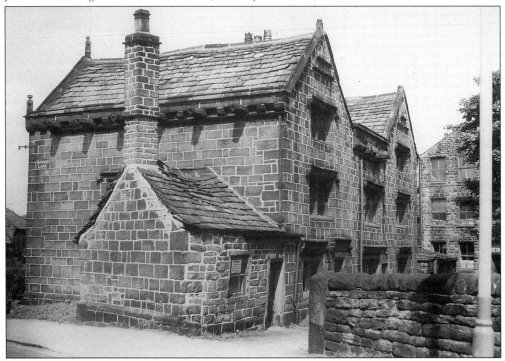

Shipley Manor House, a fine building also known as Over Hall, was home to the Rawson family, Shipley's Lords of the Manor, from the fifteenth century. It was erected in 1630 at the junction of Hall Lane and Kirkgate (on the site now occupied by the Town Hall). In 1673 it was considerably extended by William Rawson and no doubt, financed by the 120 acre farm whose estates reached all the way to Shipley High Moor.

Shipley Manor House from the rear.

16

Shipley Hall 1955. Thought to have been built in 1734 this solid Georgian gentleman's residence was located between Market Street and Otley Road close to the Market Place. At this time, shortly before its demolition, the Hall served as headquarters of the Windhill Co-operative Society, which a year later erected new premises on the site. Shipley Hall was formerly the home of Rev John Myers, a magistrate who made good use of Shipley's stocks for punishing miscreants. The stocks were conveniently located outside Myer's home at the top end of Shipley Market Place.

Shipley Low Hall in 1902. Recently renamed Shipley Old Hall but better known to today's townsfolk as the Conservative Club, this ancient hall still has an original section, the north wing constructed in 1620 (to the left of this photograph), and a neo-classical extension probably built by the Wainman family in the late eighteenth century. Prior to the arrival of the railways, it occupied a prime hill-top site with parklands and gardens running all the way down to the trout-filled Bradford Beck and as far as the Baptist Chapel. The estate was sold in 1846 to the Leeds & Bradford Railway Company for £24,000.

Bradford Road, Shipley 1904. By 1870 Shipley was a boom town of the very successful Yorkshire textile industry. After 1866 Kirkgate was quickly overrun by middle class, detached villa residences and by 1880 the Hall Royd area, pictured here, had gone some way down the same path with cheaper terraced housing for artisans. Here the recently electrified tram service (No. 172 Bradford to Nab Wood) has just passed the Branch Hotel and Selbourne Terrace on the right and Northcliffe Road on the left.

Bingley Road c. 1920. Technically well out of the Edwardian period, this photograph nevertheless clearly demonstrates how the quality of Shipley's housing stock had been enhanced by the inclusion of Titus Salt's model village of Saltaire. Here, the Bradford tram service makes a return journey along Salt's Gordon Terrace (right).

Two
Public Buildings

Shipley Town Hall c. 1932. Shipley's first modern organisation of local government was the Shipley Local Board formed in 1853. They met initially at the Sun Hotel and in 1880 leased the Manor House (on this site) for council matters and a fire station until its demolition in 1915. During the 1930s several schemes were begun to relieve high unemployment, one of which was the construction by relief workers of this stately building on the Manor House site. It was opened in 1932 by the Earl of Harewood.

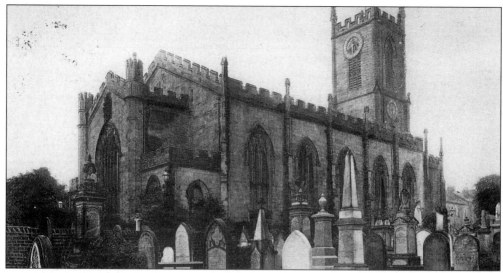

St Paul's Church, Shipley is perhaps the oldest of the town's public buildings. It was only constructed in 1826 when Shipley's Anglicans finally got their own church. Previously Shipley was under the ecclesiastical jurisdiction of the Vicar of Bradford and local inhabitants had to travel to Bradford's Parish Church if they required public worship. St Paul's was originally planned with seating for 1,488 persons. The foundation stone was laid in 1823 by John Wilmer Field of Heaton, Lord of the Manor, and was consecrated by Dr Harcourt, Archbishop of York, in 1826. Wilsden Church, consecrated on the same day, was an exact copy of Oates' Gothic style building here at Shipley. The graveyard was added in 1860 but was soon too small to serve Shipley's needs and in 1895 six acres of land at Hirst Wood were consecrated.

Bethel Baptist Church, Bethel Hill c. 1900. Shipley had no local place of religious worship until a chapel was built on this site in 1758, thanks to the evangelist Joseph Gawkrodger who first preached at the Holt in Windhill in 1750. On a prominent knoll, opposite Low Hall, the original building was extended several times as the congregation increased rapidly before 1820. Up to that time there was no baptistery in the chapel and baptisms were held in the beck at Pricking Mill or at the stepping stones on the River Aire at Dixon's Mill (Saltaire). Shipley's first Sunday School was held here in 1822. The building shown here was constructed in 1836 and finally demolished in the 1970s but the graveyard survives, leaving behind gravestones as a reminder of ancient Shipley families such as the Atkinsons, the Dibbs and the Luptons.

20

Rosse Street Chapel c. 1900. As Shipley expanded westwards over what had originally been the Low Moor (Wycliffe) area, a second Baptist chapel was built at Rosse Street in 1865 to accommodate a congregation of over 1,000 persons. Many people, including the first pastor Rev R. Greene, transferred from the overcrowded and dilapidated Bethel Chapel.

Shipley Hospital, Saltaire c. 1930. Originally, this two storeyed building built by Titus Salt in 1868 as part of his model village, had developed out of a need for a dispensary and casualty ward in Salt's mill. The hospital and its operating theatre cost Salt £6,000 but he endowed the building with an annual income and gave it to the ratepayers of Shipley who added a third storey in 1928.

Croft House, Shipley 1955. This solid farmhouse of Yorkshire stone and flags was built in 1729 at the very heart of the town. Today it is the site of the Asda store. Its garden orchards and farm lands running south as far as Shipley Fields were quickly swamped by Shipley's rush into industrialisation and urbanisation. Overrun by back to back houses such as those in the lower picture (which were immediately adjacent to Croft House) the farm quickly lost its principal function. It later served as a school, the local Labour Party headquarters and a centre for domestic cloth making. The house on the right in the lower picture is thought to have served as Shipley's lock-up during a period in the late nineteenth century. Both Croft House and these terraced, working class homes were demolished indiscriminately in 1955 and 1956.

Bradford Old Bank, Shipley branch c. 1910. The Bradford Old Bank, which later became part of Barclays Bank, was the first bank to open a branch in Shipley (New Years Day 1877). The original premises were at Stocks Hill at the top of the Market Place but just twelve years later they built these premises on the site of the junction of the Market Place and the Otley Road.

Yorkshire Penny Bank 1935. This building was demolished in 1973 to allow for the widening of Otley Road. The Bank now occupies premises in Westgate. The word 'penny' was dropped from the title name in its centenary year of 1959. In the bottom left, in the distance, is the Fox and Hounds Hotel at Fox Corner and further along were the premises of Walkers Print Works, which today is Osbaldistons, the stationers.

Prudential Assurance Company, Shipley branch 1938. This imposing, neo-classical office block was built between the wars on the Otley Road, opposite Shipley Low Hall, to accommodate the Prudential Insurance Company as well as the established family firm of Shipley solicitors, Atkinson and Firth.

Shipley Post Office, Otley Road 1900. Up to 1874 Shipley relied upon Leeds for its postal services but thereafter it acquired the status of a Post Office being allowed to sort, stamp and despatch its own mail from these premises in Bank Street (now the Shipley branch of the Halifax Building Society).

Crowghyll Park c. 1908. This public playground was opened by Mrs Titus Salt of Milnerfield in May 1890. It was laid out on land given to the church wardens in 1825 in lieu of common rights when Shipley common was enclosed. From this bandstand local brass bands performed throughout the summer season. In the background is St Paul's Church without the vicarage.

Saltaire Institute, Shipley, c. 1895. Opened by Titus Salt in Victoria Road, Saltaire, in 1871, at a cost of £25,000. For the greater part of this century it served as Shipley's main public library.

Shipley and District Working Men's Club c. 1901. The club was formed in October 1890 and registered three years later by ten founder members. In 1895, they purchased Shipley House, a detached house and its extensive grounds at Moor End (Wycliffe). By 1900 its 300 members could enjoy the reading, smoking and recreation rooms as well as outdoor activities in the summer on the surrounding park.

Butterfields of Shipley c. 1886. These are the premises of W.P. Butterfield at Windhill Bridge. On the ground floor are the handsomely fitted shops displaying the firm's lines in hardware and metal goods. Between the wars Butterfields helped to widen Shipley's industrial base away from wool as makers of industrial containers and galvanised bins. In 1937 their increased output and growing reputation warranted larger premises and they moved into Sowden's loom making factory at Low Well. The building here (only recently demolished and later known as Linley's drapery) is located at Windhill alongside the Leeds–Bradford Railway Line and the final stretch of the Bradford Canal before its junction with the Leeds–Liverpool Canal. The premises were later known as Dixon's Buildings.

Saltaire Picture House. Many of the public buildings opened after the 1914-18 War were associated with mass leisure and the cinema epitomised this trend for public entertainment. Here, the Saltaire Picture House was opened in 1922 on a site opposite the tram shed on Keighley Road. It could seat 1,500 persons and later became the Gaumont Cinema. It closed in 1957 and was demolished shortly afterwards.

Queen's Palace, Briggate, c. 1908. Formerly the Temperance Coffee House, this building became the Queen's Palace Theatre with two variety shows nightly at 7pm and 9pm. Here, there is a youthful queue for the threepenny gallery seats. In December 1915 it opened as the Shipley Picture House but was still known as the 'Old Palace'. When it finally closed in August 1932, it was immediately replaced by the magnificent new cinema of the Glen Royal, further along the road. To the right of the theatre in 1908 is Mr Lund's Fleece Inn.

Pavilion Cinema, Commercial Street, 1970. For thousands of working people the 'pictures' became a major source of entertainment after 1920. Children begged for pennies to get them into the warmth and excitement of the cinema, which also gave unchaperoned women a respectable social venue. For those who visited the Shipley Pavilion, children and adults often got more for their twopenny tickets than they actually bargained for, the cinema being well known to Shipleyites as the 'Bug Ole' or 'Bug Run'. It was built in 1912 alongside the old Corn Mill in Wainman Street. It was built and financed by an Austrian gentleman who was expatriated at the beginning of World War One.

Three
On the Move

Salvation Army Mobile Canteen, c. 1940. This gift of a van by the British War Relief Society to the Shipley Branch of the Salvation Army enabled that worthy Christian body to administer food and soup to those in need in the Shipley area during the late 1930's.

Shanks' Pony, c. 1914. While this is probably a Sunday School field day on the outskirts of Bradford prior to the Great War, it does serve to remind us that the majority of people got around their town by walking – until, that is, the arrival of the tram.

Leeds–Liverpool Canal at Shipley, 1920. The coming of the canals in the last quarter of the eighteenth century was the first real break with the past as far as transport development was concerned. By 1777 Shipley was linked with both Leeds and Skipton via the canal although the connection with Liverpool was not completed until 1816. In this boatyard at Dockfield the pleasure craft, Riocine II, is ready for launching and, in the background, a more traditional canal barge is about to be launched sideways into the water. The ivy-covered house across the navigation was the home of Shipley wheelwright, Tom Halliday.

Bradford Canal, Shipley, c. 1880. In 1774 Shipley was linked to Bradford by means of its second canal, the Bradford Canal. Here, on the last stretch of that canal at Windhill, a new cast iron bridge replaces the original stone structure (in background), carrying Leeds Road over the navigation at Windhill. The photographer is standing at the Windhill end of the canal, looking back towards Bradford.

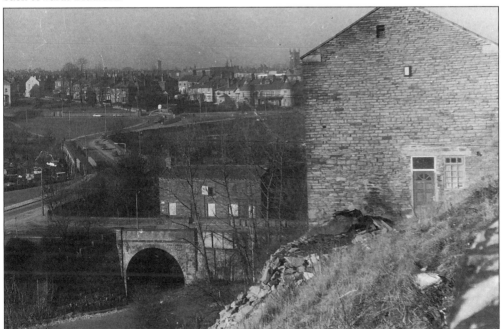

Pricking Bridge, Windhill, c. 1950. This double-arched bridge carried the road to Windhill over both the Bradford Beck (seen here) and the Bradford Canal (out of view). To the right, on Windhill Crag, is Crag Chapel (later a general store). In the far distance is the Cross Banks/Manor Lane area of Shipley.

Shipley's Canal Junction. Here at Windhill/Dockfield Lane is the junction of the Bradford Canal and the Leeds–Liverpool Canal. To the left is Dixon's Building (see No. 38) and, on the right, are the toll office and boatmen's lodging house, known as Junction house and for a number of years occupied by T. & W.H. Clark, millwrights and engineers.

Parkinson's, Shipley, c. 1980. This recent view of the offices alongside the Leeds–Liverpool Canal at Shipley can no longer be seen as the premises of the engineering works to the right have been demolished to make way for a controversial trunk road. These were the premises of J. Parkinson & Son (Shipley) Ltd., who were making looms and spinning machines in Shipley as early as 1893. In the inter-war years they became precision tool makers for a variety of British industries as well as exporting to a large overseas market. Their main products were milling machines and gear cutting machinery, but they were known the world over for their large industrial vices.

Hirst Lock, Saltaire, c. 1920. In the background is the lockkeeper's cottage and Mr Whincup's Hirst Farm. To the right is the ancient Shipley settlement of the Hyrst.

Glyn Thomas & Co. Hirst Mill, c. 1930. There had been a corn mill on this site from the medieval times and after 1700 it was converted to a paper mill by Joseph Overend whose nephew Thomas Wright built the imposing mill owner's residence adjoining the mill. In 1873 the whole site was purchased by Sir Titus Salt whose successor, Sir James Roberts leased the mill to Glyn Thomas & Company, manufacturers of flock mattresses and hygiene bedding. Mr Glynn Thomas was in business here until 1951 when he retired. It finally closed as a going concern in 1968. The mill was later converted to private flats and remains so today.

Saltaire Fire Brigade, c. 1935. The voluntary fire brigade of employees of Salts Saltaire Ltd assemble at the entrance to the mill yard of the huge manufactory at Saltaire. There, men did valuable fire-watching duties at the mill every night throughout the Second World War. The author can identify only one member of the force, Mr George Armstrong who is seated on the front row third from the left.

Midland Railway Station, Shipley in 1870. One factor more than any other made Shipley a development area in the nineteenth century, the coming of the railway. And in Shipley it arrived after fourteen years of trying when a group of Leeds & Bradford businessmen in 1844 obtained parliamentary permission to build a railway between the two towns. This was opened in July 1846 with an extension to Colne in 1847.

Saltaire Station 1953. This was part of the Colne extension of 1847. By this railway, Titus Salt was able to bring his workforce into the new mill from Bradford prior to the building of the workpeople's cottages. Here a Midland Railway Stanier Class (not named) steams past Saltaire mill and into the station in 1953. The station was closed in March 1956 but reopened in 1984.

Saltaire Railway Station, c. 1920. This photograph was taken from the bridge in the previous picture and shows the original Midland Station and bridge at Saltaire just after the First War. A train from the west is about to enter the station.

Steam Tram, Frizinghall, c. 1900. Steam trams were introduced by Bradford Corporation as early as 1884 and reached speeds of 12 mph! Here in the top picture a steam tram passes out of Shipley into Frizinghall via Bradford Road. Below a steam tram and tailer of the Bradford Tramways and Omnibus Co. c. 1887 on the Bingley Road section of the Saltaire to Frizinghall service.

Tram Shed, Shipley c.1910. This temporary structure adjoining Shipley Technical College, between Exhibition Road and Maddocks Street, was the property of the Mid-Yorkshire Tramways Company whose fleet of 10 electric tramcars was taken over by Shipley Council in 1904. These galleons of the highways, with their distinctive red livery (as opposed to Bradford's Prussian blue) operated between Baildon Bridge and the Branch Hotel as well as Nab Wood to Thackley. The Fox Corner junction with its maze of tram lines came to be known as Cobweb Square by Shipley locals.

Trolleybus in Commercial Street 1936. On 30 March 1930 the Bradford–Thackley–Saltaire tram route was converted to trolley buses and here, shortly before the Second World War, a trolleybus on that same route stops outside Fred Allsop's stationer's and fancy goods shop in a busy and congested Commercial Street. On the extreme left of the picture is the entrance to the Pavilion cinema.

Trolleybus in Commercial Street 1936. The same trolleybus service, passing the Junction Hotel, is about to leave Shipley, Commercial Street in the direction of Saltaire. A narrow Westgate leads to the Market Place in the centre. Note the cast iron horse trough on the left.

Bradford Road, Saltaire, c. 1960. The motor car symbolised the transport revolution of the twentieth century, transforming Shipley's ancient roads into congested and clogged up arteries of transport. Here, the combustion engine outnumbers people by 11 to 1.

Four
Shops and Shopping

A busy Market day, Shipley, c. 1960.

Shipley Market Place, c. 1900. For hundreds of years the Market Place had been Shipley's main retailing centre. Located at the junction of several roads and on the site of the ancient public stocks (Stock's Hill) it was from here that goods were sold and bartered in medieval times. Here at the top of the slope in 1900 is Renner's butcher's shop. Renner was a German pork butcher whose premises were attacked and vandalised in the anti-German feeling of August 1914.

Windhill Co-operative Store, Kirkgate, c. 1902. The co-operative movement made a significant contribution to Shipley's retailing revolution when the Windhill Co-operative Society was founded in 1864 by a dozen working men from Windhill each contributing one pound to found the Society in premises next door to the New Inn, Windhill. By 1872 they had transferred to Commercial Street in Shipley (Co-operative Hall). By 1885 trade amounted to £67,695 and capital to £23,785 plus numerous branches in the area. This is the drapery and footwear department in New Kirkgate in 1902.

Horne Bros, c. 1901. These two gentlemen, standing outside their Commercial Street store first came to Shipley in 1885 but three years later moved into larger premises with a canal-side warehouse to the rear in Wharf Street. From here and their Commercial Street shop they blended their own teas 'to suit the workers of the district' and roasted their own coffee on a daily basis. Here they are surrounded by a wonderful display of hams and bacon joints.

Allsop's, Commercial Street. Carefully saved pocket money enabled your author as a boy, to visit Fred Allsop's to buy foreign stamps temptingly displayed in the glass doors of the shop. Wonderful sounding places like Tobago and Gilbert & Ellis Isles leapt out at you from the enticing window displays. This family business began in Commercial Street in 1874. The original founder was Bernard Allsop (second left) a printer and proprietor of the Shipley and Saltaire Times and Airedale Reporter (1876). It was Fred Allsop (far right) the most recent owner who died in 1981, who provided this mecca for Shipley stamp collectors.

New York, Saltaire Road, c. 1965. This part of Shipley, originally the town's Moor End area, was probably named after the quarries at New York Delf. In the foreground is Saltaire Road. Extreme left are the grounds of Shipley Working Men's Club. From left to right in 1940 the shops were: Bob Scaife's (Sweets and tobacco); Dover's herbalist, York Place; Light's fish shop and Reddy's confectioners at the corner of Regent Street.

Billy Midneet's. Further along Saltaire Road (opposite today's Wycliffe CE Middle School) were the premises of William Rhodes better known to thousands of Shipley folk between the wars as Billy Midneet because of his 'open all hours' approach to business. He bought and sold anything from books to furniture. His secondhand emporium in the darker recesses of his shop was a godsend to many working class housewives in the New York area. To the right is Schofield's Yard (building supplies).

Lupton Brook's, Kirkgate Shipley, c. 1960. Famous beyond Shipley, the boot and shoe emporium of Mr Brook had its leather workshops open to public view and a claim to sell at less than cost sooner than cease to be the cheapest. In 1888 he opened a second store in Briggate but these were his original premises at the junction of Kirkgate and Market Street shortly before demolition in 1956. He was the first Shipley tradesman to install electric lighting into his shop which was also famed for its public clock. Next door is Butlands (jewellers) and Drivers (tripe shop).

Mr Lupton Brook. He was arguably Shipley's best known and most respected tradesman at the turn of the century. He had been born of poor parents near Pateley Bridge and moved to Shipley from East Morton. He first traded in Shipley's Market Place but in 1880 purchased a shop in Westgate and shortly afterwards moved to Kirkgate.

Osbaldistons, Wainman Street, c. 1953. At the junction of Wainman Street and Otley Road stands a corner shop which belongs to Shipley's oldest family retailing business. Eighty years before Johnny Walker's corner was as equally well known to Shipley folk as was Fox Corner. The site was named after Shipley's principal stationer and printer Jonathan Walker, founder and co-owner of the town's first newspaper the *Shipley Times and Express*. In 1922 Mr Walker sold out his business to Mr Oswald Osbaldiston whose son and grandson have upheld a fine family tradition as the town's leading stationers.

Smash and Grab! Osbaldiston's c. 1949. Here, Mr Harold Osbaldiston cleans up outside the family shop following a smash and grab raid shortly before Christmas in 1949 when £80 worth of fountain pens were taken by a night-time thief. Over the years the same window has been broken by a barrel of beer intended for the cellars of the Fox & Hounds opposite; smashed by a runaway car wheel and devastated by two out of control cyclists who finished up among the pens, pencils and sticking tape!

Profit Sharing Shop c. 1911. This is Mr W. Batley's profit sharing mobile grocery shop at the beginning of its round outside his main grocery store in Titus Street, Saltaire before the First War.

Shipley's Hi-tech Housewife c. 1938. Despite obvious economic problems in the inter-war years the general level of mass expectations was rising. More and more came to expect hot water systems, electric fires, wireless sets and gas cookers and perhaps even a vacuum cleaner. Here the proprietor of F.H.Somer's furniture store in Westgate presents prizes to three successful Shipley housewives in the firm's promotion of the new technology.

Mr Fred Terry, Shipley barber, c. 1960. This is Mr Fred Terry outside his barber's shop in Low Well. Mr Terry has been a barber in Shipley for many years.

Market Place, Shipley, c. 1960. This section on shopping in Shipley began with a photograph of the town's market place in 1951. How dramatically it had changed by 1961! Only Barclays Bank (left) the Sun Vaults (right) and the Town Hall had survived that transforming decade when the face of the Shipley Market Place was changed completely.

Five
Special Events

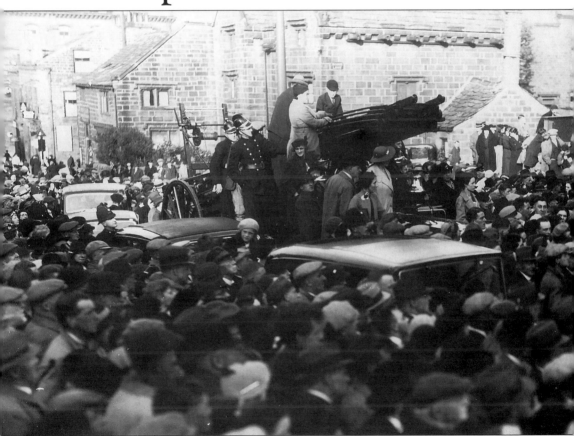

Shipley Says 'No' c. 1937. The protest march objecting to joining Bradford for local government purposes reaches its climax outside the Town Hall in July 1937. This was the third time Bradford had attempted to take over Shipley council. The strength of public outrage was measured by the size of the turn out, which was led by Saltaire Works Band and Salt's Fire Brigade.

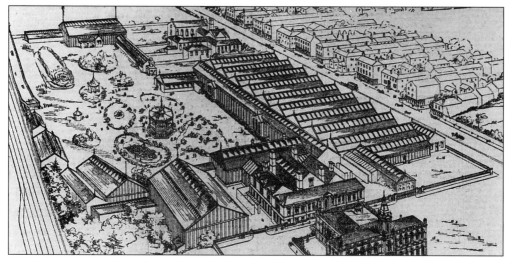

The Saltaire Exhibition c. 1887. It was really named the Royal Yorkshire Jubilee Exhibition to mark Victoria's Golden Jubilee and to raise funds for Saltaire's new Arts & Science School. Princess Beatrice and her husband Prince Henry of Battenburg officially opened the event on 6th May, staying as the guests of young Titus Salt at Milner Field. The illustration shows the nine exhibition courts alongside the road to Shipley. Victoria Hall (in the foreground was Court No. 10). The Toboggan Slide can be seen top left alongside the railway and next to it was the Japanese Village. Other features included a Working Dairy, 'Camera Obscura', a Maze and a Concert Hall.

Shipley Toboggan 1887. The Toboggan slide at the Saltaire Exhibition alongside the railway is seen in this rare photograph. In the background can be picked out Ashley Mill and the Shipley slaughterhouse. The row of terraced cottages is thought to be Victoria Street next to Henry Mason's Victoria Mill.

Northcliff Park opening 1920. In 1920 Northcliff Woods and the Norman Rae Playing Fields were opened to the public by their donor Mr H Norman Rae MP for the Shipley division at that time. Here the procession makes its way to the original entrance to the grounds (prior to the current main entrance opening in 1929). In the distance the procession leaves behind the Branch Hotel and the Prince's Hall Cinema (opened 1911).

The winter of 1947. In Shipley in 1947 it snowed on 25th January and snowed every day thereafter until 15th March. For most of that time the temperature was well below freezing; the coldest night being 24th February when the thermometer plunged to minus 29 degrees. There were snow drifts of 15 feet at Northcliff and trams and buses stopped running for most of the period causing outer districts to be cut off for days at a time. Cars and buses were buried; milk was delivered by sledge and coal and coke were at a minimum. Rationing of food and fuel returned only two years after the war. Here, mill girls take the short cut across the frozen canal on their way to work in Saltaire mill. The building to the left is the old stables and in the distance is Hirst Wood and the Salts Playing Fields.

Heavy Load, Shipley, c. 1903. This huge boiler was on the last leg of its journey from Lancashire to Shipley in 1903 (destined for Shipley's new power station) when it toppled into the canal and comprehensively sank! Here are a few of the hundreds of spectators who watched its salvage and reloading aboard 'Edith' one of several barges of Abraham Kendal & Sons, Shipley's largest canal carriers at that time. In the distance to the right, are the engineering works of Cundalls (later the Valley Scouring Company).

Shipley Horse Fair c. 1975. The ancient Shipley Horse fair retained its commercial emphasis until its very recent demise in the 1990's. Many Shipley folk will recently remember it as an Easter Tuesday treat at Northcliff but it was originally held in Shipley centre (Market Street). By 1965 it had moved to the Dumb Mill site on Valley Road. Here, in the mid 1970s there is still considerable interest as a local horseman puts a pony through its paces below Windhill Crags.

Shipley's Finest c. 1937. The final of the 'Miss Shipley' competition in 1937 was won by Miss Vida Roberts. Her attendants were Miss Doris Cawley (left) and Miss Anne Garton.

Royal Visit to Shipley 1937. 1937 was a right Royal year for Shipley with two visits from members of the Royal Family. In October the new King and Queen visited Saltaire Mill and spent time in the weaving and burling departments, talking to mill workers. Here they are seen leaving the mill.

Visit of Princess Royal to Shipley 1937. Here the Princess Royal is received in the Council Chamber of the recently opened Town Hall by Victor Waddilove, chairman of Shipley UDC. On this, her second visit to the district, she officially opened the Shipley Boys Club 27 January 1937.

'Coronation' Street Party c 1937. In May 1937 there occurred the coronation of King George VI subsequent to the abdication of his brother in the previous year. Street parties were held all over the land. Here the residents of Earl Street, adjudged the best decorated Shipley street and awarded a first prize of £10, celebrate the event 'al fresco' style. As most dads were at work the photograph is dominated by mothers and their children but the vicar of Shipley Rev Perritt and Councillor and Mrs Birbeck (back row) are in attendance. Note the wireless on the midden roof of No.43 possibly for the first ever coronation broadcast.

Six

Shipley at Work

Hirst Farm c. 1920. One of medieval Shipley's outlying farmsteads, the 'Hyrst' as it was known, was 'a myle distant from anye house of habitacioun'. Here, the barn and white-washed cottage were built at the end of the seventeenth century. The gate gives entrance to Hirst Wood and in the distance is the lockkeeper's cottage alongside the Leeds–Liverpool canal.

Hirst Farm c. 1945. This 'special' from the camera of Bill King captures the farmhouse in mid winter at the end of the Second World War with the canal property demolished and Mr Bagshaw's famous home-made ice-cream a fading summer memory. The farm and outbuildings were demolished in 1962 and the site is now a car park for visitors to Hirst Wood.

Haymaking Wrose Brow c. 1952. In spite of Shipley's status as an industrial 'boom' town, outlying farms at Moorhead and the Hirst continued a limited farming economy well into the twentieth century. Mounsey's Farm at Windhill in 1952 is a good example of this kind of continuity.

Ogden's Mill, bought originally in 1810 by William Jennings who converted it from woollen to worsted manufacture and enlarged it simultaneously. By 1879 it was owned by Jonas Ogden in whose family it remained until the 1930s. Steam-powered mills like this soon attracted operatives to live close to their place of work and worker's cottages went up all around it. In the background can be seen Dockfield Lane and the bridge over the canal.

Buck Mill, Thackley c. 1948. Initially, the local textile industry moved away from domestic/cottage production and into water powered factories (mills) around the 1790's. There had been a mill for grinding corn and a fulling mill for cloth on this site since the sixteenth century. In 1817 this water-powered mill was leased and extended by David Mellor and later used for cotton spinning and carding. The Buck Mill Bridge was opened 12 April 1889.

Victoria Mill (Henry Mason's) 1886. In his original Bradford mill Mr Mason had specialised in umbrella cloths and linings but in 1873 he moved to Shipley and erected Victoria mills to manufacture worsted coatings and dress goods. By 1930 there were over a thousand persons employed at the mill. After 1918 Henry Mason was noted for his generosity to Shipley's poor and for his daily habit of walking to work from his Bankfield (now hotel) home.

Airedale Combing Company c. 1930. On this site between Otley Road and the River Aire there have been several textile concerns of varying sizes and importance. Originally there was the Baildon corn and fulling mill in 1800. In 1850 Joshua Taylor built the Lower Holme Mills at a cost of £60,000 (extreme right). In 1856 his son Charles Frederick (C.F.) Taylor went into business in the Baildon Bridge mills (seen here immediately adjacent to the river). By far the grandest edifice on this site, however, is the property of the Airedale Combing Company which adjoins CF Taylor's mill. This was built in 1920/22 and was owned principally by Mr Francis Willey (later Lord Barnby).

Mill girls c 1932. Saltaire mill girls pose outside the public washhouse and baths on Caroline Street, Saltaire in the 1930s.

Brickworks, Windhill c. 1937. The quarry of the Wrose Brow Brickworks was located at the top of Wrose Brow Road. Here the men are manually pushing small carts to and from the quarry face.

Windhill Co-operative Society. The first shop had opened in 1864 when the working class founders opened their shop each night after the day's work was done and the men – weavers, blacksmiths and quarrymen took it in turns at serving. At the end of that first year net profits were £20 but by 1910 had risen to £25,400 – by that time the Grocery department had 20 branches like this one at Baildon Bridge (top) and the butchery department had its own slaughterhouse and 22 butchers shops like the one in Bingley Road, Saltaire (bottom) managed by John Firth (and dog!).

Shipley Fire Brigade c. 1938. First founded in 1868 with a hand reel cart and six men, this service by 1938 had a full complement of 70 men five officers and four engines housed in a brand new Fire Station (seen here) in Windsor Road.

Sowden's Loom Makers c. 1900. At the turn of the century David Sowden occupied Low Well Mill (built by William Denby & Sons) manufacturing weaving looms. Here his work force (flat-capped to a man) stand proud before their products.

Chimney Sweep c. 1900. A frequent sight around the streets of Shipley before 1900 the 'sweep' was called in once a year to clean Shipley's housing stock all of which were fired by coal. Do you remember Fred and Billy Gurney of Valley Road fame?

A Shipley Engineer at work in 1937. Engineering was Shipley's second largest industry, manufacturing machine tools, diesel engines, textile accessories, lifts, fans, bearings, clutch gears, tanks and a variety of pressed steel items. Here is an employee of J Parkinson & Son (Shipley) Ltd who specialised in milling machines and gear cutting equipment.

Seven

Shipley at Play

Bradford Road, Shipley 1935. The Shipley Carnival procession passes Northcliff and the Prince's Cinema (left).

Fox and Hounds c. 1960. Drink was an integral part of Shipley's working class culture and the public house on the street corner became a central feature of community life and leisure after 1850. The Fox and Hounds had been on this particular street corner for over 150 years giving the name to this location of the junction of Commercial Street and Otley Road i.e. Fox Corner.

Temperance Coffee Palace, Briggate c. 1900. Temperance and teetotalism was a largely nonconformist middle-class movement designed to control and stamp out the drinking habits of working people. The temperance ideal was institutionalised by a social framework of festivals, processions 'pledge' meetings, lectures and tracts. As well as Temperance Halls, premises for the consumption of non-alcoholic drinks sprang up everywhere. This building was originally the Shipley Primitive Methodist Chapel in Briggate but around 1870 became the Temperance Coffee Palace where in 1892 the Shipley Temperance Union was founded. It later became the Queens Palace theatre and cinema.

SHIPLEY SUNDAY SCHOOL SCHOLARS

Sunday School Field Day c. 1912. Whit Monday 1912 and hundreds of Shipley Sunday School scholars from all over the district congregate in the Market Place for the traditional Whit Monday Walk i.e. from their respective Sunday School to the centre of Shipley (top). Below, church leaders and a portable harmonium (!) lead the hymn singing.

Crowghyll Park c. 1910. For over 200 years this site was a quarry and Shipley's public refuse dump. In 1889 it was landscaped with terraces and promenades. Unlike the photograph on page 25 this image includes the impressive backdrop of the vicarage which was built in 1908. The level of the bandstand in relation to the church and vicarage explains the depth of the original quarry.

Shipley Carnival, Saltaire Road c. 1907. As befitted the occasion, onlookers at the Shipley Carnival in 1907 have turned out in their 'Sunday best' for this annual treat in July prior to the Shipley Tide holiday week. Even the horse is sporting novel headwear. Here the carnival passes Baker Street and Rhodes Street.

BRADFORD & COUNTY WALKING ASSOCIATION

(Founded 1903)

President: H. W. RAISTRICK, N.C.A.A.

Souvenir Programme

70th ANNUAL

BRADFORD WALK

UNDER A.A.A. LAWS & R.W.A. RULES

DISTANCE: 50 KILOMETRES

(31 miles, 121 yards)

also incorporating the
NORTHERN AREA RACE WALKING
ASSOCIATION CHAMPIONSHIP
at this distance

Starting at 9.30 a.m. prompt

from New Bank Street, Bradford

on MONDAY, 29th MAY, 1972

ROUTE		
Keighley Road	Ben Rhydding	Apperley
Branch (1½ miles)	Ilkley (14 miles)	Greengates
Shipley (2 miles)	Denton Park	Undercliffe
Hollins Hill	Askwith	Wellington Road
Menston	Otley	Peel Park
Burley (10 miles)	Yeadon Moor	

Price 5p — — — — — — — — Price 5p

Whit Walk 1972. After 1870, competitive walking or pedestrianism was taken up by amateur athletic clubs like the Airedale Athletic Club. In 1912 the Yorkshire Walking Club was formed and in 1903 the Bradford Whit Walk was first held over a 40 mile course taking in Shipley, Otley, Tadcaster and York but since 1945 the course has been a circular one (viz) of 31 miles including Shipley.

Whit Walk 1955. During the 1950s and 1960s this event aroused great interest and support from Shipley's Whit Monday holidaymakers and thousands would line the route along Bradford Road – Fox Corner – Otley Road. Here, Albert Johnson (Sheffield United) climbs Hollins Hill on his way to victory. Johnson dominated the event through the 1950s winning every year but one from 1954 to 1963. He was a great favourite with the Shipley crowds.

The Shipley Band c. 1904. It had its origins in the Shipley Temperance Band of 1890. Five years later it merged with the Saltaire Brass Band to become the Shipley Brass Band and had some success in competitions under the leadership of its conductor John Paley (a world famous cornet soloist). In 1901 the band had occupied the old Masonic Rooms in Commercial Street as a social Club.

Salt's F.C. c. 1953. The Salts Football Club had their golden years in the 1950s but their origins lie in a works team at Saltaire Mills which played on Hirstwood Road before 1914. On the completion of the Salts Playing Fields next to the River Aire the Salts (Saltaire) Football Club came into being in 1924. Under the captaincy of Fred Armstrong the club made progress in the Bradford Amateur League. By 1948 they had won the West Riding Challenge Cup and the Bradford and District Cup and had even played in the F.A. Amateur Cup. During the seasons 1950-1959 they swept all before them.

Saltaire Ladies Keep Fit Class c. 1939. Taken at the Saltaire Road studio of professional photographer, Harland Seel, this picture shows the members of the Saltaire Congregational Ladies Keep Fit Class of 1938/39. It was led by Miss Alice Pickles (centre front row) and includes her sister Miss Carrie Pickles (third from left back row) who was an international gymnast. Mrs McClellan the vicar's wife is seated in the centre.

Saltaire Boat House c. 1920. The Bradford Amateur Rowing Club had operated on this stretch of the River Aire since the 1890's and had built this boathouse upstream from the weir of Hirst Mill (and on the same side of the river). In 1920 the mill's new tenant Mr Glynn Thomas objected to the antics and noise of club members and consequently in 1922 the boathouse was taken down and rebuilt on the opposite bank of the river.

Swimming int' Cut 1936. Nothing like a long hot summer (as 1936 was) to get the locals cooling off in the canal. This stretch of the Leeds–Liverpool Canal at Hirst Wood is particularly picturesque – a veritable pleasure beach!

Shipley Golf Club c. 1920. Originally this was part of ancient Shipley's unenclosed moorland at New Close and High Moor. By 1600 all of Shipley's 'open' fields had been enclosed. Former isolated farm steads like White House and Hirst Farm were slowly drawn into Shipley's urban sprawl. Here, Hollin Hall (formerly owned by George Knowles) and Moorhead House are surrounded by suburban villas and the golf course of the original Shipley Golf Club (1897), which had a 9-hole course in the foreground.

Alan Jeffries, 1934. Joseph Jefferies was a motoring pioneer in Bradford before 1907. In 1928 his son Alan, opened his famous motorcycle showroom in Saltaire Road, Shipley. The business became famous for its sales of the Scott motor cycles which were assembled nearby in a factory off Hirst Lane 1912-1952. Here the internationally successful trials rider can be seen astride a Triumph trials bike outside his Shipley shop.

Alan Jeffries c 1930 Trialling at Kettlewell in 1930.

Shipley-on-Sea c. 1910. This is the promenade at Morecambe before 1914. It was known as Shipley-on-Sea for the number of Shipley and Saltaire folk who holidayed there. On a direct line of the Midland Railway Morecambe, received hundreds of Shipley families each year particularly at Shipley Tide Week when families queued at Shipley station for their yearly excursion trains to the seaside.

Shipley Belles c.1930. These young Saltaire girls are ready and equipped for their annual visit to the seaside. Clara and Dorothy Armstrong of Saltaire and their cousin Irene pose in a Blackpool photographer's studio – buckets and spades at the ready.

Swimming at Scarborough c. 1920. The east coast of Yorkshire was not as popular with Shipley holidaymakers as was Morecambe and Blackpool. Judging by the number of shoreline spectators mixed bathing was still something a little 'risque' in northern England at this time.

Shipley Fairground c. 1955. This should bring back happy memories for many Shipley children of the 1940s and 1950s. Every Easter, Marshall's fair would suddenly shoot up on this waste land site between Otley Road and Union Street whose back to back cottages ('the Square') can be seen in the background. To the right is the chimney of the old brewery at the rear of the 'Old House at Home' pub.

Shipley Fair 1938. All the fun of the fair for a penny. That is the cost of this children's ride at Shipley Fair at Easter 1938.

Glen Royal Cinema/Bingo Hall 1983. Opened 5th September 1932 this luxury picture house replaced the dilapidated Palace also in Briggate. It was built in red brick by a consortium of local businessmen including Liberal Councillor Clifford Cawthorne and Mr Hyde. It was Shipley's premier cinema during the great cinema age of the 1950s. Those Shipley cinemagoers who preferred the circle to the stalls will remember the mysteriously illuminated figure of a Buddha halfway up the staircase. For those youngsters who survived it, the Saturday matinee was a nursery for future cinemagoers (Oh Happy Days!). It was converted to a Bingo Hall in 1963 and finally closed in 1982.

Glenroyal Cinema c. 1936. All the Shipley cinemas installed organs in the 1920s. Here we have Lupton Brook Jnr, at the console of the 2 manual La Fleur electronic Hammond Organ installed in the cinema in 1936. This luxury cinema could seat 1,100 people and had opened with the film 'Emma' starring Marie Dressler and had closed in December 1962 showing 'Mix Me A Person'.

Saltaire Brass Band 1937. The brass band movement has its oirgins in the Sunday school and temperance movements but after 1850 local mill owners and employers also financed works bands. Shipley's reputation in this field was high with Hammonds Sauce Works Band and this, the Salts Mill Band sporting their recent success in the national competition of 1937. Here they are resplendent in their brown and yellow uniforms on the steps of the recently opened Shipley Town Hall.

Shipley Dance Band c. 1938. Between the wars, tastes in popular music changed owing to the popularity of the wireless and dance crazes from across the Atlantic. 'Swing' music did not pass Shipley by and here, Horace Healey and his Blue Military Boys, were just one of the numerous local bands to entertain the young people of Shipley at venues like Fred Town's Dance Hall or the more salubrious Victoria Hall.

Shipley Water Polo team 1938. Shipley's new public swimming baths had been built behind the Town Hall in Manor Lane in 1930. Six years later the Shipley United Swimming Club entered competitive water polo leagues in Halifax and Leeds. In only their second season of competition they were runners up. Here the team is captained by R. Smith. On the back row, in the collar and tie is the baths manager, Mr B. Isherwood.

Ring O' Bells 1938. These 'Ring Raggers' of 1938 had entertained crowds throughout Shipley Carnival Week, raising funds for local hospitals and charities. The pub probably derives its name from the fact that it stands within earshot of the bells of St Pauls' Church in Kirkgate. At this time the pub was part of the Melbourne Brewery (Leeds) taken over by Tetley in 1960.

'Laikin Aht'. Not all leisure was organised and commercialised and for many working class children, like these, when school was finished and the chores done, boys and girls made for a favourite manhole, lampost or street corner to play spontaneously a variety of catch and chase games in which their imaginations could run riot over 'cops an' robbers' or 'cowboys and indians'. Gang domains were clearly marked and not to be trespassed upon unless by the local 'rozzer' (policeman). These youngsters on Leeds Road are clearing rubbish on a demolition site, probably for a fire.

Hirst Farm c. 1939. A location fond in the memories of many Shipley people who liked to stroll through Hirst Woods or along the canal bank before 1960. In the years on either side of the Second World War, this eigteenth century farmhouse with its stepped chimney stack and white-washed walls became a popular refreshment point for ramblers and weekend walkers. Farmer Whincup, pictured here on the extreme left, was the first owner to offer jugs of tea and home baked scones during the 1930s. Later, George Bagshaw was more famed for his home made dairy ice-cream, and his bamboo fishing nets for catching 'tiddlers' in the canal.

Eight
Shipley Glen

Shipley Glen Pleasure Grounds 1950. It was the Baptist minister Rev Scott of Bethel Chapel, Shipley who first drew public attention to the pleasures of this natural beauty spot. Traditionally it was known as Brackenhall Green and located wholly in Baildon not Shipley. In the 1840s Rev P. Scott brought his Sunday school scholars here for their annual excursion and so began its reputation with Shipley and Bradford pleasure seekers.

Temperance Coffee House on Shipley Glen. Scott's temperance ideals soon took hold among the rocks and woodlands of the Glen's geography. The Walker family who had owned the ancient farm on Bracken Hall Green since about 1630 (seen here on the right) quickly converted an old cruck house outbuilding (left) into a refreshment room for Rev Scott's visitors. By 1885 under the ownership of Thomas Cooper it had assumed the grand title of the British Temperance Tea and Coffee House (also selling ginger beer and offering overnight accommodation to tea parties). Old Tom Cooper (pictured here) sold medicines and herbal coffee from his large herb garden until finally the lord of the manor evicted him.

Shipley Glen c. 1910. The large irregular shaped boulders of Shipley Glen are the creation of the Ice Age; sandstone debris dumped by the moving glacier as it retreated in the warmer climate. Here visitors relax between the rocks and enjoy a place of great natural beauty. In the distance can be seen the sprawling suburbs of Shipley as they overrun Saltaire into Hirst Lane and Tower Road.

No. 9 Rock on Shipley Glen. Many of the large rocks overlooking Glen Beck (Lode Pit Beck) have been weathered into some unusual shapes, e.g. here is the infamous No. 9 Rock, a huge overhanging boulder of millstone grit beneath which, it is said, an illegal gambling school assembled in late Victorian times; but better known to more recent generations as a rendezvous for desperate lovers.

Bracken Hall Green c. 1900. So popular had Shipley Glen become by 1900 that it figured in music hall songs, dialect poetry and local tram and train timetables. By 1900 the Temperance Cafe had been replaced by the premises shown here (left) and the new occupant William Marsden opened a small menagerie and exhibited monkeys in the building to the right.

Ocean Switchback c. 1900. Marsdens' menagerie was little to compare with the entrepreneurial ideas that Sam Wilson had for Shipley Glen. In 1888, in a field alongside Bracken Hall Farm (left) he had erected the Ocean Switchback, a big dipper type ride.

Bracken Hall Farm 1930. By the '30s the commercial potential of Shipley Glen had gone but it remained as popular as ever with visitors. Here the old farmhouse is derelict and in the foreground can be seen the remains of a carriage of the old switchback.

Shipley Glen Tramway 1895. Another of Sam Wilson's initiatives for the Glen was his tramway of 1895 (top). This cable hauled carriageway brought visitors to the Glen up through Walker Wood for one penny and returned them at the end of the day for only half a penny. In its heyday, as many as 17,000 visitors used the tramway in one day.

Toboggan Slide on Shipley Glen c. 1900. Two years after the Glen tramway was opened, Sam Wilson (seen here) built a spectacular slide described here as 'the longest, wildest and steepest toboggan slide ever erected on earth'. It ran from the edge of Brackenhall Green down the steep slope of the Glen and part way up the other side. Riders travelled individually in small cars and were then returned collectively in larger cable hauled toboggans. On Whit Sunday in 1900 a cable snapped and a car ran back to the bottom, injuring five people. Wilson immediately closed and dismantled the ride.

Japanese Gardens Shipley Glen 1904. Even the residents of the area began to cater for the thousands of summer visitors to the Glen. Thomas Hartley built, in the gardens of Ivy House, a series of concrete gothic arches (in miniature) around which flowed a ten feet wide watercourse upon which flat bottomed boats would take customers on a two circuit ride amid the beautiful landscaped flower beds.

Japanese Gardens c. 1904. The rough and unusual appearance of these fantasy arches and structures was achieved by Hartley's use of the clinker and ash taken from Shipley's steam trams. It is intriguing to realise that a Japanese Garden, Toboggan Slide and Camera Obscura were all features of the Saltaire Exhibition of 1887 and within a decade were all found on Shipley Glen.

Aerial Flight Shipley Glen 1890. This was built by two local men, Messrs Halliday and Badland in 1889. Passengers were transported in a suspended cable car along the edge of the Glen from Bracken Hall Green to Old Glen House. Here a cable car is about to leave the station of the Aerial Flight.

Pleasure Grounds at Shipley Glen c. 1950. To complete the pleasure park of Shipley Glen are the amusements and rides in the grounds of the Vulcan House (1879) at the terminus of the Glen Tramway in Prod Lane. These were opened by J.W. Perry in 1892 and run by Bradford publican, Mr George Voss between 1915 and 1938. It was he who opened a small zoo and menagerie here and after 1945, the new owner, Mr Harry Teale rebuilt many of the rides including the Aerial Glide.

Gypsy Encampment at Shipley 1937. Holiday makers and visitors to the Glen in turn attracted travelling gypsies who would make their camp on the Glen (top) and stay the whole summer. In 1937 the gypsy Petulengro boosted local carnival funds by organising and staging his own coronation as King of the Gypsies and by staging a traditional Romany wedding between his nephew Leon Petulengro and Eileana Smith. Both occasions were open to the public and 200,000 people were estimated to have visited the Glen that summer.

Nine

Schools and Schooldays

Shipley Central School, Standards 7 and 8 Boys c. 1928.

Windhill Wesleyan School 1889. Prior to the great Education Act of 1870, Shipley's elementary school provision was a voluntary one from five main schools: Valley Road and Saltaire factory schools; Shipley and Windhill church schools and this one – the Windhill Wesleyan school. It was built alongside the chapel (later Windhill Mission) in 1849. Here, well dressed boys and girls of Windhill working class parents pose with their teachers Miss Woolley and Mr Needham.

Shipley Central Board School c. 1900. The Act of 1870 created school boards with the powers to raise rates and build new schools. Shipley's school board was elected in 1874 under the chairmanship of Titus Salt (junior) and its first school was the Shipley Central School (1876) in Saltaire Road, under the headship of Mr Morrell. It is now called Wycliffe Church of England Middle School.

Woodend Board School c. 1890. This school had been opened at the bottom of Leeds Road, Windhill in 1885 as part of the Idle School Board but with the amalgamation of Shipley and Idle in 1895 it became part of Shipley. By 1901 Shipley had 3,758 elementary school places of which 3,168 were registered.

Woodend Board School staff 1910. Headmaster Richard Dennison had been in charge of the school since it opened. Here he sits (centre) with his staff and pupil teachers at the school's silver jubilee celebrations in 1910. Mrs Firth, to his left, was the headmistress of the infant department and was one of over a hundred teachers employed in the Shipley Board's Day Schools in that year.

156. Children at Crag Road School in 1914. Shipley School Board also acquired the premises of this school on Windhill Crag when it amalgamated with Windhill in 1895. The school had opened in 1891 and in the summer of 1914 Miss Louisa Gelder, headmistress, was an advocate of the principles of 'open-air' teaching. Pupils cultivated vegetables and flowers on small plots of land. Here they enjoy a traditional ring game in the school grounds before lessons begin.

Salt's High School 1895. Built by Sir Titus Salt in 1868 as an elementary school it was given by him to the Shipley Board on condition that it became a High School offering secondary education. As forward thinking socially as he was commercially, Salt offered to replace this elementary school with another in Albert Road, Saltaire in 1878. After some doubts, the Board finally opened this school in 1877 as a High School for 11 - 15 year olds with a system of scholarships available for the pupils attending any of the Board's elementary schools. Suddenly an educational ladder was available to Shipley's working class children.

Saltaire Road Girls' School 1937. Salt's ideas of a two tier system of education were finally adopted by the state in the Hadow report of 1926. Shipley U. D. C. quickly adapted the system to the whole district. The High School at Saltaire continued to offer an academic curriculum at secondary level. After 1927 an enlarged Otley Road School became Shipley's selective central school providing courses of a technical and commercial nature. Woodend and Saltaire Road became Senior Schools for unselected 11 year olds. Here girls of the Saltaire Road Senior School celebrate the 1937 coronation in the school hall with their teachers led by Miss Trueman the headmistress.

Shipley Central school team 1921. The Central School in Saltaire Road offered its pupils a wide variety of physical activities, particularly after the war, which had revealed the poor physical condition of English youth. Here the senior boys soccer team pose in the school playground.

Saltaire Congregational Sunday School. Before the rush to state education began in 1870, the Sunday School movement had been an important provider of literacy for many poor children. This large and stylish building was provided by Titus Salt in 1875 shortly before his death. It seated 800 pupils and had separate entrances for boys and girls. The site had been reserved for a hotel but the idea was abandoned. It was a great pity that such a fine public building (the last to be built in Saltaire) had to be demolished in 1973, to make way for yet another car park.

Shipley's Open Air School 1937. Shipley's go-ahead education authority completed its local system with a new nursery school at Hirst Lane (1930) and the Baker Street Infants School (1935). Here, in September 1937, is their special needs provision, the opening of an open air school at Heaton Royds for 80 pupils at a cost to the ratepayer of £9,000.

Ten
Between the Wars

The centre of Shipley in 1935.

Shipley Market Place. By the middle of the twentieth century Shipley's Market Place geography had changed little from the Edwardian days. The Sun Hotel continues to tower over the site and the pork butchers are still in the same premises, though the stocks and public fountain have gone. In the lower picture of 1957 the arrival of the automobile has made the site congested.

Kirkgate 1936. By 1935 Anchor Stores, haberdasheries and general drapers, had occupied the premises on the corner of Stocks Hill (now the Cricketers Public House). Across the road, Lupton Brook is still selling footwear and next door is the Star and Garter public house. The sign to the Co-op Cafe is pointing along the passageway leading to Spurr Road and Market Street.

Fox Corner c. 1945. The other main focus of Shipley's urban geography in the Edwardian period had been Fox Corner and so it remained. The hotel still dominates this busy junction with Osbaldistons below in Otley Road and John Drivers grocery store next door in Commercial Street. Across the road, Rimmington's the chemist has moved into the corner premises.

Otley Road c. 1925. A photograph taken from Briggate about 1925. The two figures outside the stationer's shop (left) are Mr Osbaldiston and his son Harold. In the centre is the Reliance garage (later Ellis Brigg's bicycle shop). Between them and adjoining the canal was Sunderland's greengrocers. To the right is the corner building of the Midland Bank with the Registry of Births and Deaths on the second floor.

Otley Road from Baildon Bridge c. 1935. Further along the Otley Road this time and looking back from the recently widened bridge towards Shipley. On the right is C. F. Taylor's Airedale Mill and Sutcliffe's furniture makers occupy the former iron foundry. To the left are the public houses of the Airedale Hotel and the Bradford Arms.

Branch Hotel, Shipley c. 1950. Officially Otley Road begins here but the road leading off to the right was always known as Shipley Lane Head and the pub as the Coach and Horses or John Crabtrees. Behind the pub is the Prince's Hall cinema and the large building in the distance is Hall Royd Methodist Church built in 1937 at a cost of £7,000.

These buildings and the rows of terraced houses behind them, Regent Street, Thompson Street and Wycliffe Street had accommodated Shipley's expanding population after 1870. Far left is a corner of Saltaire Road School, more affectionately known as 'Bugville College'. On the right Billy 'Midneet's' shop. On this short stretch of road were four public houses – the Victoria, the Alexandra, Prince of Wales, and the Woodman.

Nab Wood/Moorhead, Shipley c. 1935. As land came onto the market after 1880 the Nab Wood and Moorhead areas of Shipley were developed for middle class homes. Abraham Kendall was a canal carrier in Ashley Lane and Wharf Street in 1900 but living in Park House he owned most of the Nab Wood estate and prior to 1914 built detached villas in Kendal Avenue and Grove, Bromley Road, Highfield Road and Parkfield Road. Between the wars semi-detached housing shot up all over the New Close and Nab Wood area. To the right, the once isolated Hollin Hall and Moorhead Farm are confronted by surburbia.

Shipley's new Town Hall 1932. The Shipley Urban District Council came into existence in 1894 having 15 councillors and the growth of the township in the twentieth century has largely been to their credit. As early as 1898, the population of Shipley had reached 25,000 and the rateable value had reached £100,000. After 1901 the U. D. C. bought out the local gasworks, widened most of the principal highways; built new tramways; opened a sewage and refuse plant at Dockfield; built several new schools; implemented the Public Libraries Act and obtained a ready supply of water for the town. The opening of this building by the Earl of Harewood in 1932 epitomised Shipley's success story.

The Shipley protest of 1937. In this year the Bradford Corporation made its third attempt to take over Shipley council. This came only seven months after Shipley had sought Borough status for itself. Opposition to the merger was widespread. Here the protest march, led by the Saltaire Brass Band and the Fire Brigade approaches the new Town Hall in Kirkgate. To the left, at the end of Manor Lane, is Shipley Old Hall and in the distance is the Star and Garter pub. In 1974, after local government reorganisation, there was no such outrage and Shipley went like a lamb to Bradford's slaughter.

A Shipley family c. 1919. When long-time Shipley resident George Armstrong returned from his long and terrifying stint on the Western Front he had lost a teenage brother, numerous pals and he had seen little of his family. He was promised a 'home fit for heroes' but the inter war period was one of social breakup and economic readjustment. These years brought no solution to the problems of life in a swiftly changing world. There were no incentives and people like George and Sarah Armstrong resigned themselves to surviving and coping with life as best they could, from day to day and getting as much pleasure as they could from their children.

Woodend Homes c. 1929. At least George Armstrong kept a job and a roof over his head in the years between the wars. Most unemployed people continued to occupy the working class housing left over from nineteenth century – two up, two down terraced houses like these in Woodend with outside privies often shared with neighbours and a tin bath filled from the 'copper' in the kitchen.

Party time 1937. Life was not all doom and gloom and for the youth of the inter-war years life was still to be enjoyed. After all, they were in tune with many of the new forces of change, cosmetics, shorter skirts, motor cars, cinemas and swing music. By the generation who had made it through the war, young people were admired simply becaue they were young ! Here a mixed party (with alcohol) celebrate the coronation of 1937 amongst the looms and machinerry of Henry Mason's weaving shed.

Eleven
Shipley in 1955

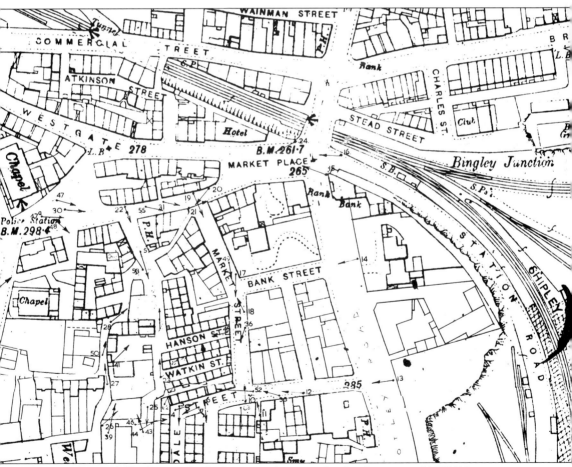

A map of central Shipley as it looked prior to the central redevelopment of 1955/56.

Shipley before....

Thanks to the photographic skill of Bill King we can compare the impact of the re-development programme on the centre of Shipley. In the first picture of 1947 the central township is dominated by the Wellcroft Mill and the back to back terrace homes of Union Street. The Baptist Chapel and Town Hall are also prominent.

....and after 1955.

Fifteen years later and the mill has gone; much of lower Kirkgate and Market Street have been replaced by the new shopping precinct and the Union Street slums have disappeared. Shipley U. D. C. threw itself into the clearance of sub standard nineteenth century housing even before 1939 and by 1970 had demolished 2,900 such houses. After 1945 the infamous Square in central Shipley became a prime target for clearance and in the process of doing so the heart of the old township was ripped out and completely replaced.

Shipley redevelopment 1955/1956. All the buildings in the following pictures were demolished in the redevelopment of the central area: Kirkgate's Star and Garter pub has sold its last pint; to the right is Croft Street leading to Croft House; below is Spurr Road with the side entrance to the Star and Garter; ahead are the back to back houses of Hanson Street and Hudson Fold.

Market Street in 1955. The first photograph shows a view along Market Street in the direction of Kirkgate; to the right is Bank Street and Shipley Hall; below, looking back along the same street with Cryer's joinery on the right and the gable ends of the terraces in Hanson and Watkins Streets.

Kirkgate in 1955. Firstly, a view of the junction of Kirkgate and Market Street showing Shipley Hall and Lupton Brooks; below, looking from the same junction towards Otley Road and the Market Place. In the background is Stead Street.

Market Street 1955. In the first picture we are looking south along Market Street towards Bagnall paint stores (left) and Firth's florist shop (right).

Market Street 1955. Firth's shop is now on the left, immediately adjacent to the narrow passage leading to Spurr Road.

Bank Street 1955. A view across Otley Road up Bank Street with Shipley Hall (Co-op) on the right.

Bank Street 1956. Just one year later – on the left is the old post office now occupied by a building society; in the distance is the chimney of the public baths.

Union Street, looking down Dale Street towards Otley Road with the entrance to Union Street on the right. The building with the hoarding is Bagnalls; next door is a dance hall which adjoined the Ministry of Pensions Office. The tall building on the right is the Old House at Home pub.

A view southwards along Union Street towards Cross Banks.

The gardens of Croft House 1955. Hudson Fold is on the far left with Dale Street on the right.

A view down Well Croft Street towards the present Market Place; Hudson Fold is set back by the lamp post.

Union Street 1955 looking
northwards. Beneath the line of
washing, youngsters are collecting
'pennies for the guy'.

These three storeyed back to back
houses were part of Shipley's
notorious 'Square'. Salem Chapel can
be seen in the background.

Windsor Road and Manor Lane c. 1965. A second phase clearance of sub standard housing close to the town centre took place in this area in 1966 allowing for the construction of a supermarket, library, swimming pool and health centre. Here are houses in Windsor Road and Wilmer Road shortly before their demolition.

Low Well c. 1968. The Bradford to Kendal trunk road (A650) travels through the township and road widening schemes in the early 1970s on both sides of the town eased considerably the congestion at peak times. Low Well is not the bottleneck for traffic it once was.

Fox Corner 1974. The widening of Briggate and Commercial Street meant saying goodbye to some old friends: 'Bug ole' Allsops, Musical Union, Midland Bank, Fox and Hounds Hotel, and Fox Corner itself. Osbaldiston's now has pride of place replacing Fox Corner in deed but not in name.

Shipley Market Place c. 1965. The clearances of the 1950s left the centre of Shipley completely transformed. A fine new market square flanked by new shops and incorporating a bus station – all overlooked by an impressive clock tower. Here, service 66 (Windhill Crag) arrives at the terminus.

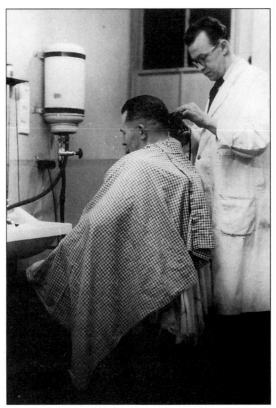

Bill King in 1955. The final section of this book is dedicated to the memory of W. F. 'Bill' King, who took most of the photographs presented within this chapter, and many more besides, of his adopted community of Windhill. Bill was Suffolk born in 1906, but was brought to Shipley as a baby by his parents who began a horse hair business in Wharf Street. Living in Baker Street, Saltaire he met and married Emily who worked at the mill there. They settled in Windhill in 1931 where Bill spent the rest of his life working as a foreman engineer at Parkinsons. He took up photography as a teenager with a box Brownie and from the 1930s he kept a pictorial record of his changing environment, developing and printing his own black and white (never colour) photographs.

At 82 he joined the Windhill Memories Group and they published a book of Bill's photographs of old Windhill. The success of the book made him a celebrity on the local lecture circuit. Sadly, Bill King passed away in 1993 at the age of 87 leaving behind a wonderful pictorial record of his heritage, his beloved Windhill. Here Bill has a haircut in Tommy Rhodes' barber shop in Otley Road, Shipley in 1955.

Twelve

Windhill

Windhill Crag c. 1820. Windhill took its name from a hill and a cottage built on the rocks at the junction of Airedale and Bradfordale. The cottage was located upon the lateral moraine of Millstone Grit, an impressive range of rocks overhanging the valley of the Bradford Beck. The area backed by thick woodland was once a romantic and picturesque spot. It was also known as Gawcliff Crag, an ideal home for rabbit, fox and other game as late as 1810. At that time Windhill consisted of no more than a dozen cottages with its main highway, the Crag Road, leading from the tiny hamlet at the Holt to open land beyond the Primitive Methodist Chapel (Rochester Street).

Windhill's fortunes prospered with the local woollen trade and caused a dramatic change in the hamlet in the late eighteenth century. Early clothmakers including Verity's of Windhill Hall; the Skirrows of Wrose; the Hallidays and Denbighs of the Holt. These men worked their wool in their own looms and carried their goods to the cloth halls in Leeds twice a week. Large scale manufacturing came with the conversion of the old Pricking Mill alongside the Bradford Beck. Thereafter other mills followed, many of them close to the Bradford or Leeds–Liverpool Canals. The owners of these mills brought much prosperity and change to the community at Windhill. They included William Jennings, James Rhodes and Sammy Cowling who married the daughter of Jeremiah Kitson.

Windhill Crag c. 1935. This photograph is taken from Carr Lane (from left to right the mill chimneys are 1, 2, and 3,). As early as 1890 the tearraced housing of Fair Bank, Annie Street etc. had covered the Crag to the left of chimney 1. Immediately to the right of this chimney is Crag Road School (now High Crags School) built in 1891 and Pratt Lane. Between chimneys 2 and 3 are the council houses of Prospect Street built shortly before the photograph was taken. To the right of chimney 3, in the distance, is Shipley centre with Wellcroft Mill and Union Street quite distinct. In the far distance are the open playing fields of Northcliff and Heaton Woods.

Windhill 1947. A later view of Windhill from the Northcliff playing fields showing the community nestling beneath the heavy brow of the Wrose escarpment. The chimney (top right) belongs to the Wrose Hill brickworks approached by Prospect Mount. In the bottom right hand corner can be seen the huge sandstone rocks of glacial debris which gave the place its name and sitting proudly upon them the little green wooden hut of cobbler 'Sammy' Cawthorne. Over to the left is the mill chimney of the Wrose Brow brickworks.

Windhill Crag 1947. A more southerly view of the Crag from the Northcliff playing fields showing Carr Lane in the top left hand corner and Crag Road running across the middle of the picture; between them are the terraced cottages of Fiddler's Green, along Hollin Lane; at the centre of the picture is the Royal public house with Holdsworth Street to its left and Stubbing Road on its right. Looking towards the far right, along Crag Road is Windhill Primitive Methodist Chapel (1886) and Crimshaw Lane.

Crimshaw Fields, Shipley c. 1935. Crimshaw Lane once led to Crimshaw Fields and is one of the most ancient parts of Windhill. After 1600, these fields were often in the possession of the Kitson family. Simeon Kitson was Windhill's leading farmer and clothier in the late eighteenth century. Towards the bottom of the photograph can be seen the Three Rise Locks of the Bradford Canal (1774); and in the bottom right corner is Owlet Grange; top right is Wrose Hill Brick works whose employees lived in the terraced houses of nearby Hollin Lane.

Crimshaw c. 1920. This ancient farmstead was one of the the outlying farms of old Shipley (Windhill). By 1920 country ramblers from Shipley and Bradford could obtain afternoon teas and fresh dairy ice cream from the farmhouse (left) which still stands in amongst a 1950s housing estate. The whitewashed cottages had been demolished by 1945. To the left, are the woods and orchards of Owlet Grange.

Owlet Grange. This solid Victorian residence was derelict for most of the author's boyhood (1955-1970) and remained so until it was converted in 1988 into six flats for the homeless at a cost to Shipley U. D. C. of £100,000. Back in the 1840s it was occupied by a well established Baptist family from Wrose, the Wilcocks.

Gawcliff Crag. So named, after these large rectangular blocks of millstone grit (left) over-hanging the Bradford beck below. Pride of place on the skyline belongs to All Souls Church Mission and behind it, Crag Road School.

Diggers Hill c. 1950. These steep, well worn steps led down from Crag Road into Diggers Hill and then to the Canal and Pricking Mill (1770) in Windhill Briggate. The diggers referred to are the gentlemen who emptied the 'nightsoil' from privvies and closets of the houses on the Crag and consequently old Crag-enders had a less complimentary name for them ! The Steps themselves were known locally as the 'catsteps'.

20

Briggate, Windhill 1890. Diggers Hill led down to Briggate. Note the sheer rock face of Windhill Crag on the left; top right and in the distance is Somerset House, Otley Road; to the rear of these houses was the Bradford Canal, the Midland Dyeworks and the goodsyard of the railway. In the house above the archway in 1891 (House No. 105) lived a brickworker, Solomon Heath, his wife and their five teenage children (four of whom were working). For Solomon and his family this back yard was an important place in working class family life. Firstly, it contained the closets (note the outbuildings) – the only place where individuals could be assured of a little privacy; it also offered a sanctuary for younger children from the rough and tumble of street life. Here, father cobbled and sawed; older children kept rabbits and pigeons. The Whittakers and Butterfields living next door brought a strong sense of real neighbourhood.

Briggate c. 1933. Crag Road eventually joined Windhill Briggate opposite Cowling Road. Further along Briggate, heading in the direction of Woodend is the New Inn (far left), which is next door to Mr Garnett's joinery and Mrs Long's haberdashery; far right is Seaton's fruit and vegetable shop.

Briggate Windhill c. 1933. Directly across the road from the previous photograph were these forbidding premises in Water Lane. The steps led to an unoccupied club room and the house on the right is the home of the shroudmaker Mrs Brook. The slip road and fencing (left) led down to the canal side on Dixon Street where Mr Harrison had his plaster works.

Water Lane, Windhill 1933. The previous photograph was taken from outside Chambers grocery store seen here. The shop is in Briggate and next door was Stott's fish and chip shop. Both of these photographs were taken by Shipley's planning department with a view to clearing sub-standard housing in 1933. The Second World War intervened but the fate of these buildings was sealed.

Carr Lane at Windhill c. 1910, taken from outside the Blue Bell Hotel at the junction of Carr Lane and Briggate. It was obviously a favourite meeting spot for children of the Holt (immediately to the rear). The Holt was perhaps Windhill's oldest settled site but by 1910 it was the centre of a working class community whose members were mostly textile workers employed at Perseverance Mill just opposite.

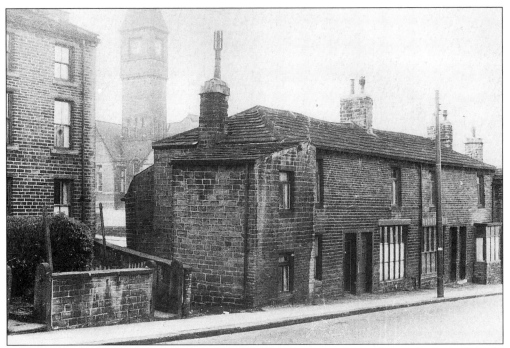

Leeds Road, Windhill c. 1960. A row of very old houses across the road from Ogden's Mill. At the side of this row the ginnel led into Wrose Brow Road. In the background was Windhill's most famous landmark, the Board School clock which was erected in 1885 by the Idle School Board. This school later became a senior school for Shipley.

Leeds Road, Windhill c. 1910, the main road eastwards out of Shipley and Windhill. Here, before 1914, an electric tram travels on the Saltaire to Thackley service; to the right is the Alma pub named after a Crimean War battle of 1854 and therefore built in the 1860s like the back to back housing surrounding it.

Leeds Road, Windhill 1954. Looking towards Thackley, the Alma pub is seen here on the extreme right. Wellington Street post office is distinguished by the large hoarding for Player's cigarettes. The street, at one time, had been the childhood home to the celebrated Oxford linguist and professor, Dr Joseph Wright; next to Woodville Street is yet another branch of the Windhill Co-operative Society. Each of these streets had a shared outside closet accommodation at the north end.

Dog and Gun Inn, Windhill c. 1955. This old Windhill pub, a favourite with those in Woodend, could be found between Mellor Street and Wilcock Street and across Leeds Road from the Alma pub.

Windhill from Wrose Brow Wood 1952. Behind the linear industrial development of Leeds Road and the urban in-filling of old Windhill and Woodend there still survived a more traditional way of life. Here, on a summer evening in 1952, haymaking goes on at Mounsey's Farm which supplied the people of Windhill with most of their milk and dairy needs well into the 1960s. However heavy industry was already on their doorstep in the form of Lee and Crabtree's (Metal Box) machine tools (centre).

Windhill Tarn c. 1908. Here is the tarn at Wood Top, a favourite winter haunt of Woodend children. The houses, top left, are in Valley Street with Princes Street in the centre; the Pit House is in the foreground; the chimney of Lower Holme Mill at Wood Bottom can be spotted in the distance.

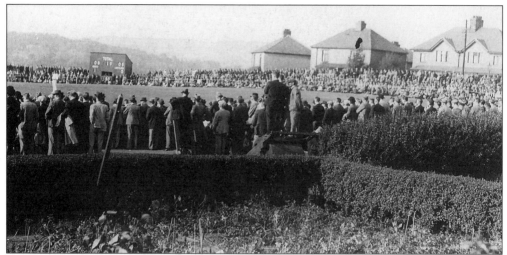

Windhill Cricket Field 1941. Only four years earlier the club had opened their new clubhouse but it was nowhere near big enough to contain a crowd of this multitude – here just to watch a weekly Bradford League fixture ! Today the Yorkshire County Club would be envious of this kind of support. The Windhill club was one of the first Bradford League clubs to sign up star professional players. In the years before the war Leary Constantine, the great West Indian all-rounder, played several seasons for the club.

A last look at Shipley and Windhill 1961. Although most of central Shipley is out of sight behind the trees (left), this is an appropriate view with which to end the book. To the right of the tree is Francis Willey's massive Airedale Combing plant and running across the centre is the Shipley to Leeds railway line. Windhill's best known landmark – the Board School clock tower is just to the right of the chimney of John Smith's jam factory (1865-1971) and on the right of the picture is Ogden's Mill and Wrose Brow Road.